Misterioso

MISTE

RIOSO

Poems by

Sascha Feinstein

COPPER CANYON PRESS

Printed in the United States of America.

Grateful acknowledgment is made to Sascha Feinstein for the use of Anita Askild Feinstein's artwork on the cover.

Copper Canyon Press is in residence under the auspices of the Centrum Foundation at Fort Worden State Park in Port Townsend, Washington. Centrum sponsors artist residences, education workshops for Washington State students and teachers, blues, jazz, and fiddle tunes festivals, classical music performances, and The Port Townsend Writers Workshop.

LIBRARY OF CONGRESS CATALOGING-IN-PUBLICATION DATA
Feinstein, Sascha, 1963-
Misterioso : poems / by Sascha Feinstein.
p. cm.
ISBN 1-55659-136-5 (pbk. : alk. paper)
1. Jazz – Poetry. 2. Jazz musicians – Poetry. I. Title.
PS3556.E435 M57 2000
811'.54 – DC21 99-050996
CIP

9 8 7 6 5 4 3 2 FIRST PRINTING

COPPER CANYON PRESS
Post Office Box 271
Port Townsend, Washington 98368
www.coppercanyonpress.org

1999 Hayden Carruth Award

The Hayden Carruth Award was established in 1998 to honor the most distinguished first, second, or third book manuscript from among more than one thousand annual entries received at Copper Canyon Press.

ACKNOWLEDGMENTS

These poems first appeared in the following publications:
American Literary Review, "Corcovado."
American Poetry Review, "Portraits and Ceremony."
Cloverdale Review, "The Long Walk."
Colorado Review, "Summer Cremations."
Confrontation Magazine, "Singapore, July 4th."
Crab Orchard Review, "Anders and the Norns" and "Mango."
Crazyhorse, "Above and Below the Surface," "All the Scars," "Blues Villanelle for Sonny Criss," and "Sienna Blossoms."
Denver Quarterly, "Misterioso" (section II).
Green Mountains Review, "Blues for Zoot," "Buying Wine," "Isis," "Miss Brown to You (1915-1959)," and "Summerhouse Piano."
Hayden's Ferry Review, "Amulets" and "Sonnets for Stan Gage (1945-1992)."
Missouri Review, "Misterioso" (section I).
New England Review, "Christmas Eve," "*Coltrane,* Coltrane," and "December Blues."
North American Review, "Misterioso" (section III).
Ploughshares, "Ruby, My Dear."
Southern Poetry Review, "*Il Cristo velato.*"

"Blues for Zoot" was reprinted in *The Note.*
"Blues Knowledge" and "Christmas Eve" were published in limited editions by The Bookcellar in Bloomington, Indiana.
"Blues Villanelle for Sonny Criss," "Blues for Zoot," "Singapore, July 4th," and "Summerhouse Piano" were reprinted in *American Poetry: The Next Generation* (Carnegie Mellon University Press).
"Misterioso" was reprinted in *Black Music Research Journal.*

Some poems also appeared in a chapbook titled *Summerhouse Piano* (Matchbooks, 1989).

I'd like to thank several writers who, in different and essential ways, influenced this collection: Jerry Ramsey, Tom Gavin, Sena Jeter Naslund, Maura Stanton, Yusef Komunyakaa, David Wojahn, and G.W. Hawkes. "Misterioso" is for Yusef; "Corcovado" for David. Some poems were written with the aid of Professional Development Grants from Lycoming College. I hope Hayden Carruth realizes that his selection of this manuscript has made me feel like the Prazedint ov the Wuurld. Finally, a few of these poems speak about my father's life, but all of them were shaped by his philosophy of painting, and by the paintings themselves.

for Marleni, Kiran, and Divia

Even today, when a child cries at night, he is taken outside and shown the stars. "There is your mother," they say, "the place we all come from and where we all return, and there is no need to weep."

– Lawrence Blair on the Balinese

Monk's always doing something back there that sounds so mysterious, but it's not at all when you know what he's doing. Just like simple truths.

– John Coltrane

Contents

Misterioso

i

"Coltrane, *Coltrane*"

His white-horse sleep can't be seen
on record, though Monk's double
call, loud at first, then softer,
propels him to his feet, galloping into

"Well, You Needn't." Water and God
will clean Trane's body by the end
of the year, '57, but now only
Monk's voice cuts through

the drug's pull: his mouthpiece
locks against rotting teeth,
sound responding in a flurry
on the beat. It's a strong solo

but not his best, not quite up to
what would come. Ten years
before his death, he's thirty-one,
just four years older than

I am now. The tape clicks into
auto-reverse, and as I drive past
Indiana's busted red barns
the album cover comes to mind:

Monk's checkered cap, dark green shades
with bamboo at the side, natty black suit,
kerchief in the pocket. On his lap,
sheet music atop an attaché case,

and he's crouched into a child's
red wagon, halfheartedly holding
the handle. He was thirty-nine.
His tilted head and time as seen by

an almost-dead cigarette lets us guess
he's had enough takes for one day.
When my friend John turned the same age –
two years before his body stopped holding

the daily quart, bloating like someone
drowned, before he dried out for good –
I gave him that record. All evening
Monk and Trane played backup

to trays of heavy crystal clinking
Jack Daniel's on ice. A nickel-dime
poker game in the corner with less
at stake, it seemed, than John's

articulately slurred argument, fate
vs free will. His art students,
some said in the morning, did well
before they switched to ouzo.

I'd left by that round. Lily,
my date, wanted some air, to walk
by the Ipswich River, then the graveyard
because, she said, there's no better relief

for the August nights. She took me
to the moonlit Mayflower stones,
our fingers inside the mossy-etched slate
to feel a time that had passed.

We crossed a path of pine needles,
tall cedar trees, some fallen
by the winter's blight, thick
and tangled wood filling the air

with carmine scent. It was there
she told me what happened to her
as a child, how her mother must have heard
father closing one door, then the other.

What could I tell her?
When I touched her hand, she kissed me
on the mouth, said she was sorry,
it was the drink, that she'd ruined

the evening and please not to think
less of her. Most had fallen asleep
when we returned. We left some people
in rocking chairs, a cardplayer

on the couch, the carpet patterned
with arms and legs like a Caravaggio,
varnish darkening as we turned off
Noguchi lamps, the overheated stereo.

Driving alone to Thelonious's septet,
I often wonder if she ever made it
South, summer in New Orleans, her paisley
blouse catching smoke, blues bands

outside the French Quarter:
shadows of trombone slides and clarinets
muting their solos across her eyes.
Before she drove away, I held her

close enough to feel against my face
her hair, curling and smelling
sweet, almost like the vapors
of whiskey, almost like cedar.

Sonnets for Stan Gage (1945–1992)

Your hands cracked and callused in summer, bled
Every winter. *That's the way it's always been,*
You said, clutching your fingers in a mottled
White towel. All of your unspoken
Words – the angular elbows and snapped wrists –
Resonate in memory like cymbals left
Unstruck, forever anticipating the stick's
Crash. Damn it, Stan. You thought death
Was some young drummer you could cut, the way
You kept outplaying fate with heroin
Overdoses, a mugger's four-inch blade
In your chest which now I can only see in
My mind heaving. The clean linoleum tile.
A nurse washing her hands. The cold bed rail.

Floodlight shadow. Your shoes are stroking
The platform's edge. Two hours before the gig –
The drums HAVE *to be intimidating!* –
And because you think they're not you take a swig
Of J.D. from a shiny flask. But they were.
This was pain: each platinum strike drove nails
Into my head. ("STAN!") I'm still caught there,
Pressed against the auditorium wall,
Twitching as warm-up shots detonated
My chest. ("STAN! You've made the clock jump
Forward!") *Yeah, but did they* INTIMIDATE?
Sticks on the drum-kit rug, you walk to the front
Of the stage, fingers slicing the air,
Flicking blood across a row of wooden chairs.

With young people the heart keeps beating even
After other organs decay, your mother told me
In the hours when tubes of pure oxygen
Failed to purify your liver, your kidneys –
Just days after being admitted, amused,
Almost, that you'd finally quit smoking. (And what
Hipster wrote, "Drummers and poets are used
Like ashtrays YES"?) I loved how with cigarettes
You'd sketch Emily Remler's guitar solos
At Fat Tuesday's, and you wanted every note
She played. *Can you believe it? Thirty-two!*
("Was it a heart attack? Someone wrote –")
No, speedball. Impish smile. *But okay, sure –*
I mean, you know – EVERYONE *dies of heart failure.*

I expect to see at dusk your rhythmic
Figure strutting Main Street, on the way
To some "no cake" gig, shades and hair slicked
Clean as your black suit, your grin – *Hey, babe!* –
And news of a book on the twenties
Art scene in Paris. You'll tell me you're sure
I won't believe it. And you'll tell me jazz
Is just another language for the curve
In a woman's dress photographed from behind.
And look at this. And look at this. And look
At this. But right now I can't even define
What loss feels like. Sycamore leaves. My rake
Scrapes up fallen sticks. I feel my dry skin
Chafe from the air. My hands are bleeding.

Blues for Zoot

They had crew cuts then, puffed cheeks like kids
spitting water: Al Cohn and Zoot Sims spouting tenor saxes
on the cover of *You 'N Me,* my dad's original pressing;

I hoped they'd sign it. Zoot clouded the room,
smoke fading his face, milky freckles. In five years
he'd die of cancer, and maybe he knew, maybe I knew,

because instead of looking into his eyes, I stared
at his shoes, then thought of the Kenton band, Zoot forgetting
to wear socks one night, how Stan said he'd have to leave

if he couldn't dress right. Next gig: still no socks,
and Zoot – he rubbed shoe polish on his ankles. Backstage,
when I met him, his pant legs hung too high, and I could see

blue socks, even a hole, his striped pants thin and washed-
out. Al put his horn down, scribbled his name, walked away.
But Zoot checked out the tunes and brushed his fingers

across the photograph. He said, *Man, this is old,*
and I thought he meant, *Where'd you get it, kid?* I told him
my father's name, Provincetown summers, the fifties,

how they'd play softball. Zoot closed his eyes, hard
to think back so many years, until, looking up somewhere
in the room, he said, *Oh yeah.* I'm not sure what I wanted

to hear, perhaps just my father's one-liner, *Good-tempered*
stuff, and lousy playing. He'd talk about artists, sculptors.
When Mulligan or Sims played the A House,

Dad would say, *they'd hit with us,* and I'd always ask for
the Zoot story. *Herman Cherry pitched that day,* he'd begin,
Franz Kline at first, Sims led off. From the bench,

Mulligan yelled, "Give 'em Hell!" so Zoot smiled, and Herman
picked up a softball. He'd pause as though he needed to,
ask if I wanted to hear it all again. *We had painted*

this grapefruit with white acrylic, black scratches
for stitching. Herman lobbed it slow, a moonball,
and you could see Zoot's eyes get big. Then he really

connected – THWACK! We'd laugh, his hands rapping
the table. *There's this burst of fruit and juice,*
little pieces of white paint sailing down the third-base line!

Zoot just dropped his bat and said, "Shit" – he rubs
his hands and laughs, glances at the liver spots
on his knuckles, and says, *You should have seen his face.*

When I met Zoot Sims twenty-six years later, I wanted to ask
if he remembered the sound from that day at the plate.
Or how it felt to be one of the Four Brothers. Instead,

I watched his pen sign the photograph, his fingers holding
the jacket for a last look. *Here,* he said, *collector's item,*
and before he turned, reached out for his yellow horn,

I shook his hand. Christ. What else was there to do?

December Blues

As though drum rhythms could sort it all
out, I'm listening to forties records, Count
Basie, and Jo Jones on drums, a tired blues.
Jones brushes a beat, the sound of

boots slushing through old snow. Somewhere
in Philly they're burying my grandmother,
a second stroke at ninety-four, eight years of lost
memory, and though it's the bluesy horn section

I usually hear, today it's the steady
push of rhythm. The evening I heard Jones
live – The West End: Harold Ashby on tenor,
an Irish fellow on piano – he kept laughing

at nothing in the crowd, his temples seemingly
collapsed, operating shadows. I got a free bourbon
for good nature, but when the pianist hit
two notes to pass the time, Jones screamed,

Shut up! I told you to shut up years ago.
Ashby looked across the club with a *fuck this*
glare. Someone dimmed the lights. Then Jones
laughed like an owl and clicked into an easy

swing rhythm, the high hat shimmering a pulse.
A night of short sets, lulls, Jones cutting them
off with his loud snare until Ashby said, *I don't*
need this shit, man. Who does he think he IS?

The last time I saw my grandmother she couldn't
recognize anyone. Patients slippered across
white linoleum toward windows and doorways.
My father's face, my face: I became her son

in 1934, memory like perfume
for ten minutes of lucidity: *Remember*
the cantor in our town, the one with the walk?
It was cold outside. He knocked on our house.

We made him some tea, laughed with him, and then
he sang for us – she hummed a clear melody,
and I believed her when she said
his voice was more beautiful than summer.

Blues Villanelle for Sonny Criss

A lunar eclipse, and your solos spread
across wild clover as I exhale
and try not to think of the gun at your head,
how we say but rarely believe, "You can't be dead

if you're on record." Your alto wails
to the moon's elision, the solo spread
against the splintering woodshed.
It's '57, one year before jail,

twenty before the gun's at your head
and you're my age playing "Calidad,"
"Willow Weep for Me," "Love for Sale,"
as the brief clips from your solo spread

the graying moon like cigarettes
in walnut-paneled dives, overpriced cocktails
cold as the gun you'll hold to your head.
But I'm trying not to see that, trying instead

to let the bass and chromatic scales
eclipse you, solo, outspread.
I'm trying not to think. The gun's at your head.

All the Scars

– for Thorpe Feidt

If evening light crosses their eyes
or shadows an earlobe just right,
we can tell them apart.
The thinner twin can't quite articulate
all he wants, though he's the first
to look at your painting and see spirits
breaking from the rocky soil
to indigo sky, vertical white flashes
reaching beyond the frame's edge.
In this triptych, the central body
with arms above its head
in a celestial leap
has eyes almond shaped
and the twins can sit for hours, thinking
not about their fatherless childhood –
of the man who drove his sons
to Florida's Disney World,
gave them the ride of their lives
and vanished in the crowd –
but of orange rocks, vermilion fires,
vast hills with peacocks
and lavender houses, volcanic ash,
the immense black cloud dissipating
to God's bitter smile, and whatever it is
that white light leads to. The spirits
have no mouths, and I went slack jawed
at these images in your studio,
having driven from the Cape
and a night on a chaise longue
listening to Anne speak of two lost hours:
The blackened back roads

of South Yarmouth where she braked
for brilliant columns, then a swirling skirmish
flooding an almost-midnight sky.
No streetlamps and just one house
charred to the beams and boarded up.
She stepped from her car,
checked for steam on the road.
"Come back. I've seen you."
Shadows of two telephone wires
and nothing more.
But at home, she caught the hands
of the kitchen clock, gripped a chair's back.
So much time elapsed. "I used to cry,"
she said, "when people didn't believe me."
Then, cold as stone, "I don't anymore."
Through hypnosis, she saw the overwhelming
pink light softening silver
edges of glistening tools,
all the scars doctors can't explain.
More visitations, more inversions
of time, and she'll never understand why,
when they placed icons around her table –
We won't see you for years –
she collapsed into vertigo, a sadness
deep enough to be death,
her slender arms sweeping across leather,
and the hypnotist couldn't leave her there:
Come back. Right now.
What images she retained,
three, he made her draw and, reaching
for their perfect union in a locked file,

smiled by closing one eye.
"When sunsets turn peach," Anne told me,
"I start to shiver." I thought
I could rise into the stars
until they bespangled my body
with the night's current.
Whom do we become after we've been
explored, losing memory?
The twins hypnotize themselves
to your painting's journey
and ask each other about flight –
how many ghosts filter across
the triptych's landscape,
where they come from, what
they reach for. The boys want answers
I don't have. Below, in the rock,
there's a cow skull burning in lava,
or perhaps it's the large socket
of a fish eye fossilized in a river's
surrender to mountains. But most often
it's another spirit enjambed in dirt,
splinters of shale and blasted granite
imprisoning its almost-white arm.
Burnt sienna head, no mouth,
no ears, no eyes. Without a crevice
to release some force that will rise
into forms we acknowledge
yet cannot with precision distinguish,
this is what the stone holds.

Miss Brown to You (1915–1959)

Nobody, you once wrote, *really loves me.*
They just love my music. I'm listening
to the end of your life, sessions
from '58, and forgive me for thinking,
That's all I have, Billie.
Because you were right. I'm not the woman
in this photo, signing autographs
behind the enormous letters
of your name. To your left,
one of the men checks to see
if you've spelled his right;
another watches your downcast
eyelashes. I wish I had a moment
like that to remember you by, though
with "Don't Explain," I'm sent to a blue room,
your scratched voice like winter wind
under the door, pushing forward.
There are days, Uncle Bob once told me,
I listen to Bach and it's so perfect
I can't hear anything else. Except Billie,
of course. You might have answered, *Honey,*
I'm flattered, but I ain't perfect.
If it were '58, you'd probably give a wink
to the rhythm section, sing
for everyone you thought didn't love you
and for people, I'd like to believe,
not yet born. But if it crossed your mind
later, you might think about perfection,
all the things you had to become
for others: "restricted" diners flashing
the bus window pink, how even
Basie once asked you to wear

brown makeup, skin not dark enough,
the backstage mirror reflecting your white
gardenia as fingers slowly spread
the new color across your cheek,
red lips seeping into the darkening rouge.

Buying Wine

His alto leaks steam, a radiator of sound,
frozen breath shining on the bell. He's good,
and I can't help but lean against the bus stop

and watch: someone's blue cotton hat with
a Yankees sticker not doing shit for heat,
cut-open gloves to finger the horn, a raincoat

from the Salvation Army, and two blocks up
some fellow stuffed in a Santa suit clangs
for donations. There's a fluorescent haze

from the local food mart, carts for bags no doubt
full with fatty hams and cranberry relish,
sweet potatoes, flour for the thick gravy

and scones, tubs of butter, peaches, fresh
cream. The wheels scrape icy concrete, clatter
quickly by him, somehow blending with an off-

minor run so hip I yell to him, *Do it, do it.*
A hunched figure sorts his change, drops coins
that vaguely catch the light. I've got

seven bucks for a Chianti, bills twisting
in my pocket. When I return with a bottle
he's playing "Blue Monk," slow for the mood,

just up enough for circulation. I empty
what's left so fast he knows I can't be
counting, knows it can't be much,

but pulls the sax from his mouth to thank me.
Wonderful holiday to you, sir. I wave,
and only when I reach the apartment

do the sounds disappear completely. You're
basting a roast, and my ears fill with blood.
We kiss, I pour the wine, and of course

it's delicious. *I'm so glad you went out*
for this, you say. *Everything's just perfect.*

ii

Amulets

Here, careful with the edges: 1922,
Bucharest. That's my father in light pants
cut at the knees. He's almost seven.
His brother, age four, between grandparents.
Three cousins – he's the one who dies
in World War II – parents, uncles, aunts.

They lived in a town between Kiev and Odessa
near another that flamed the hillside,
and the soot speckled my grandmother's apron
as she and her aunts quietly sewed
rows of gold coins, like points on a map,
into their children's knickers,

then wrapped candlesticks in burlap
to mute starlight at the border where
guards held paper bills over gas lamps,
checked for pinholes. *You won't need this.*
Open that, please. Five dollars for water,
much more to cross the Dniester

at gunpoint, and in the morning bandits
on mules abducted the women,
packed them in an earthen room
until my grandmother offered three pendants.
If anyone was hurt, no one speaks of it now.
For months they worried about my great-

grandfather's clubfoot and Ellis Island.
Potato soup tasting of soil, songs
to keep warm, then Romanian sleet.

So they photographed the family and left
by rail to Hamburg, across the Channel,
six days on White Star Lines' *Olympic.*

I'm told one great-aunt saw stewards chewing
gum and thought they had palsy. Her sister
stared at celery and tried but couldn't quite
imagine flowers for dinner. Another, the eldest,
almost died. Dad remembers how
storms dragged the ocean through the air.

No scarves or hats waved at Liberty
against Manhattan's drizzle.
Without a cane, my great-grandfather
covered his right foot with children
tugging the leg while he laughed at fear.
They changed his name and let him through.

My father looked up at a woman in uniform
who smiled and extended a glowing hand.
He'd never seen an orange before, rolled it
in his palms, smelled his fingers, bit into
rind, then flesh. His first memory of
America: the color and taste of gold.

Christmas Eve

You'd think they'd be with family,
At a party, out of town, but it's Miles,
Monk, Bags, Percy, and Klook
In Van Gelder's New Jersey studio.
Twenty-five years later, I fall for
A woman who has both out-of-print LPs,
Together a collage of tunes
From that gig, two cuts of "The Man I Love"
With a mumbled argument that stops
The first take. We tried so many times
To make out the words, unable to hear
Enough through her speakers, pressing together.
Young love. 1954: my parents
Hadn't met, couldn't imagine
The failure of their first marriages
Or why my mother would turn to painting,
To my father's classes, their attraction
Unspoken. Love came to them the way
Miles punctured the air with notes soft enough
To hold a woman, lines floating somewhere
Between Jackson's vibraharp mellifluous
Against Monk's dissonant chords. Late
December. I won't be born for nine years.
It's the holiday, though Dad doesn't know it
Yet, that deadens what's left of the marriage,
Days he won't talk about unless
Memory triggers a joke: what not to say
To a wife, how not to listen when you should.
This is the holiday my mother decides
She won't return to the U.S. until
Divorce papers arrive signed, but comes back

For reasons she doesn't understand,
Facing it. Streetlamps on her lost complexion.
And who decided to tint the black-and-white
Cover photo of Miles with eyes closed, horn
And harmon mute now sickly fluorescent?
No snow in Hackensack, but it's cold and
Monk's pissed 'cause Miles asks him to lay out
During trumpet solos. They have words.
Some in the studio leave for dinner
And don't return, regretting forever
Not hearing live the improvisations
That swelled from angry respect and need.
Across the Hudson, my father attends,
By himself, a party in the Village.
My mom's there also, though she's with the husband
She doesn't want, hangs her head
Until hair hides her face, and my father
Doesn't even see her. I wonder, sometimes,
What he would have said, what she would have heard,
If she could have answered at all and could he
Withstand pockets of silence the way Miles
Did not: the second take of "The Man I Love"
Where impatience and Thelonious's time
Cause the trumpet to enter midchorus.
Monk hammers the bridge, consumes the space,
Cuts him. It's more volatile than their fight
On the first take where Bags pedaltones
The intro, his phrases fracturing
To Monk's mutiny, momentary chaos:
"When you want me to come in, man?" and
"Man, the cat's cuttin' the thing," and
"I don't know when to come in, man," and

"I stopped too, everybody –," then Miles,
"*Shhhhhhhhhhh,*" hushes the group, and because
He knows for some reason this is important,
That it's part of what makes the music, turns
To the booth, to Van Gelder nervously
Recording the gig, and says, "Hey, Rudy,
Put this on the record – *all* of it."

Summer Cremations

1. Cape Cod, 1980

Kiln fire burned the vase indigo
        like a night sky waiting for stars,
                what my father had hoped to see

in brushstroked snapdragons
        and irises. A sentimental inscription,
                and I'm glad he didn't read it

in the eulogy, his friends standing
        on the sun-bleached deck, rising and falling
                with a pulse of the tide. He spoke instead

of Mother's weavings, how she had touched
        other worlds through color and form –
                the urge, journey. In the distance,

the breakwater's thin gray line misted
        into a sleepy wash of coast. He paused
                and I thought of the midnight sun,

woven Scandinavian myths
        of Odin and Freya holding each other
                in Asgard, or the eight-footed horse,

Sleipnir, who raged through Nordic ice.
        Some of her tapestries sold
                long ago. He tilted the urn

into winds that lifted her ashes
across the bay. Behind the large boat
lulled waves of lilies, roses

from her garden sparkling the current,
and when a seabird circled the cluster
one close friend said she was with us.

I don't know if I believed her,
but I watched the bird become a cloud
while the petals withdrew.

II. Bali, 1987

They had mourned a full year and now
even the widows smiled, settled
the bones wrapped in cotton cloth

into hollow bellies of wooden bulls,
horns and white faces
in the forest of relatives

and strangers. Sun so hot, I wondered
if the red and gold paints would melt
into wood, or if the less elaborate bulls

with straight unpainted necks, mounted
like broken posts from an ocean jetty,
would collapse. A boy with a kris

sold iced coconut water, and I recalled
        the words my father said as I left him:
                Walk with the gods. Suddenly a priest

waved his arm, summoned torches,
        and in minutes straw sparked into flame
                twisting through wooden legs, straining

to reach the necks. Strange dragons:
        mouths half-open as they exhaled
                wasps from a burning nest.

I stepped back. The smoke sent me farther,
        mist welling in circles like a chant,
                and my eyes closed. When they opened,

animals had lost their skin,
        though the hanging trees never caught fire.
                In the air, dissolving clouds turned

orange with the sun, souls dancing
        their patterns on the sky,
                half-moon, the Southern Cross.

Sienna Blossoms

She'd peel and press garlic cloves until they salivated into the burn,
a witch's trick she learned in Malmö, '47, the year that boy she loved
tried to grasp lingonberries and paralyzed his hands with hornets.
Even today I'll watch my skin swell to iron filings, the venomous surge,
disbelieving the moment the way my father stood in the doorjamb,
his cottage bedroom where my mother barely slept the year before.
He held her ashes, and I thought when his hand covered his mouth
he was caught in time. But no – What found its way into the room
was a rose vine, firm as dried coral fans, arcing deep sienna blossoms
above the dresser mirror. We followed young thorns to the abandoned
wasps' nest, the perfect hole in the shingles where in a spring freeze
the vine must have tasted brackish pine air, dipped its head,
leafless and slick, curved into warmth, slid beneath mossy parquet
where it pushed and unglued masking tape, and then drove to eastern light,
flowering in its salvation for weeks, perhaps, before the leaves turned
soft and gray. My father severed the stem flush to the plaster, pulled gently,
and spent his summer upturning black soil with lemon rind and herbs.

Anders and the Norns

– for my mother, Anita

The fairy tale wrote itself from a dream,
you said, and your illustrations bloomed
to the cover: my middle name,
Anders, in tall letters circled with blue.

Above the mountains, three Norns
whispered as they spun the lifelines
that guide our journey. One night, a storm
swept the peaks, whirlwinded their twine

into hard knots: a child born backward
in manners, stuttering, though he sang
his youth with the forest's birds –
tanagers, parakeets, toucans.

Coming home one day, he saw black wings
and a huge beak pulling the line's end,
took hold of the last knot, and, flying
now, soared over houses, an ocean.

They glided to an island called *Wish*
where he met a king and his daughter
who had chestnut-colored skin. The princess
untangled the line until his stutter

disappeared, and they fell in love. Anders
made a wedding dress for her sewn
from the island's large white flowers,
and she wove a suit from his own yarn.

After you died, we packed the book away
but I've wondered as the years passed
how you could have known that day
what I couldn't have known to ask:

Did you see my future appear
in the vision before your death?
For I'm in love with a woman whose hair
drifts down her back like tapestry threads,

her skin dark brown, her home an island
halfway around the world. In dreams
she's curled her fingers into your hand,
the two of you rising over vast green seas.

Above and Below the Surface

A dragon spits the rusted dart
to sell itself and mahogany Śivas
drip their stain, so I vanish
in shallows far from tiger sharks,
the barnacled wharf and floating pylons
singing the rhythm of this tide.

You emerge in a lotus blossom
of Indian Ocean, rivulets
from your mouth to breasts,
a braid over one shoulder, the sea
brittle and brilliant in your thick hair
as mirrored hands dry your lashes...

How startled you would have been
to see me so close, if I had waded
one stroke beyond your dive, if
this story were exactly true.
We did not meet in Southeast Asia
or your mother's village near Madras.

Should I describe that summer
without storms, the stunted ears of corn
lining southern Indiana highways?
I sat in a half-moon of students
glazed in dreadful realities,
silent as the inside of a fish,

and from the amphitheater's crest,
late because the sun should rule time,
you dipped your head below
the low drone, invisible
until you rubbed a pear's red blush
and kissed its skin to your tongue

as the flesh gave way, remember?
The chairs folded into themselves.
The chalk returned to the earth.
The moon eclipsed the room
but not your eyes, and not my hello,
and not the rain that let me hold you.

Mango

– for Divia

My wife sifts through dry rice ripening a mango,
breathes the blushed skin with the conviction of time
and the knowledge of green. *One more day,*
so she buries it again. Outside, sisters from Sri Lanka
carry you through the garden while they comb your hair.

Two years ago, we thought you'd slip from the womb,
but today they build a levee of pillows
on the bed where you were conceived,
turn off the light to cool the room, your face
a pearlized flush of tropical air.

Portraits and Ceremony

– for Kiran

Coriander and Thai chilies seasoned the flesh
of a black chicken we had carried alive – bagged,
feet bound with yarn – from one peak
to the next, where a family lined a wall

with wet clothes and led us inside
their home. The grandmother kneeled
by a star-shaped fire and lit
a sloping silver pipe. *Thank you.*

Please. We shared five or six words.
The rest: universal or unknown,
for what has poetry to do with rice fields,
with water buffalo that till the soil,

or that pig lashed to a tree, fattened
to be slaughtered for a wedding
or sold should the crops fail? Its gruel boiled
before sunrise, smoke waking two boys

who cut our plastic water bottles,
carved wooden wheels and axles
for dusty drag races. Our guide said,
Her eighth and ninth child,

and she became turquoise and magenta
when he pointed to their dance. Hand gestures –
I have two children – and when I showed her
a photograph of my son

she held it to her blouse and asked
with her eyebrows if it was for her.
Can I admit to you what I tried
not to show, that handing her the image

made me sweat? That night the floor
seemed to press into my back
like the essence of distrust. Spirits
and rituals. Impossible to think

she could value a picture of my child
simply because I had kept it dry
in the rain forest. How deeply
she nodded in the morning

when I asked to take her portrait.
Son, even if you were old enough
to climb those hills, I could not tell you
what streams we crossed

to find her. Open
the photo album with silver lettering.
She's the woman wearing a cloudless sky
and six strands of crimson beads.

iii

Corcovado

1. Antabuse: August 12

Even behind glass it curls to sepia,
        this photo of her husband, Stan Getz,
                in '66: from the beach house she clicks

precisely at midleap, thinks, *He's a*
        dolphin, then removes chilled orange juice
                thick with pulp, crumbles Antabuse

that floats and dissolves. Underwater, Stan
        replays his June gig on the South Lawn
                with Johnson, who's booked him for Thailand

come October. The sand turns mescal
        as he squints for Monica, thinks, *She's gone,*
                leans to shore, to a young woman's towel:

dried starfish. Later, in a catamaran's
        wake, she'll smile *yes,* and he'll open her hands.

II. Palace Debut: October 23

The Queen smiles when he says *Yes,* opens his hand
and folds his fingers in time: *two, three, four...*

Roy Haynes brushes bossa nova and Stan
leans into melody from '64:

"Corcovado." She mouths the words, so he quotes
Astrud's phrasing – *Quiet thoughts and quiet*

dreams – until sandalwood and jasmine
in the ceiling fans bewilder geckos,

caress the elephants' sewn mirrored skin
the way stars in Ayuthaya beckon

palace spires. Vibraphone: *Quiet walks*

by quiet streams, and a window that looks
out on... Cigarettes discolor pink scallops.

Stan chain-smokes a blur of boyish good looks.

III. Gold Leaf: October 25

Chain saws of smoke, the tuk-tuks blur gridlock
        as car horns, come-ons, and saffron priests
fuse in the visible heat of Bangkok.
        The broken air condenser's thin white wisps

fail to cool. *All day,* Stan thinks, *I've swallowed*
        salt. What Third World–, then: *Phenomenal*–
The Reclining Buddha shimmers in shadow,
        its footprints spiraling mother-of-pearl.

Jesus, he says. *You think I can play here?*
        The guide says nothing, walks off and buys gold
to anoint the smooth torso. Monica

slips one sheet into Stan's palm, a prayer.
        Hours later in his suite, he unfolds
onto his horn gold softened with vodka.

IV. Round-Trip: October 27

Monica's voice softens as golden Scotch
refills the pewter mug that will shatter
a bathroom mirror when
                he catches
her palms clouding a blazing shower
with Thai heroin. For this
                she'll ache
all week as she extracts thatch from the room
divider. Stan flies that night
                to JFK
via Hong Kong, Tokyo, Bombay, Amsterdam.
Jet lag and layovers:
                he debates
leaving the scene, letting down LBJ,
books the return flight when he lands.
                No sleep,
but he arrives an hour before the State
dinner. The Queen glances at his shadowed jaw:

What hours you musicians must keep.

v. State Dinner: October 29

For hours the musicians keep
calling, and they're stunned to see their leader
beneath a garuda as he borrows reeds
and a horn from King Bhumibol. *My tenor's*

broken, Stan says. They talk of Goodman.
Haynes repairs a dented skin. Steve Swallow
from behind the bass: *Good to see you, man.*

The trio plays "Lush Life," "Fine & Mellow."
I'm sorry, Stan tells LBJ. *My wife's*
got some stomach bug. The air turns green
curry, mutton, coconut, sambal, lime.

Real good, but dangerous, you know? He
hooks the horn, slices mango to cool Black
Label, tightens the strap, twists the neck.

VI. Palace Garden: November 5

Bhumibol loosens the strap, cleans the neck
and mouthpiece. Later he calls LBJ
to learn where Stan buys his horns. (*This Vietnam*
PR, Johnson tells an aide, *has gotten way*
out of hand.) Two Selmers on Pan Am
arrive by December, but this week
the King gardens and dreams bossa nova.

A servant brings water and papaya.
He reclines beneath a thatched pagoda,
brick walls showering bougainvillea
as he leans over scalloped orchid beds
and pours his goblet around a bright
hybrid he's named for his wife, Sirikit.
To play like that, he thinks. *Just for one night.*

vii. Salle Pleyel, Paris: November 13

The quartet's booked for only one night.
Burton, Swallow, and Haynes watch the wings: Stan's

hypnotized by the smoke dance of Scotch through
soda, cut glass he carries to the stand.

(Applause.) On the & of four, the first note:
"When the World Was Young." No one else solos.

The vibraphone floats and dissolves in the sparse
bass line, mother-of-pearl spiral...

Monica untucks the hotel's blue sheets,
imagines "Quiet Nights of Quiet Stars"...

The festival erupts. Stan raises his crystal
to three women waving, wets his reed:

"Desafinado." (Applause.) Cameras
flash his glass, ice curling to sepia.

Misterioso

I.

One-fingering my way through
the White Pages I stopped
upon T.S. Monk, dialed,

and when a voice deeper
than mine would ever get said
Yeah I said nothing

for several seconds.
I've blocked out my nervous
words – something about

digging your music, until
a laugh said, "Hey, friend –
you talkin' 'bout my father."

You were in retirement then,
dying before I could see you
though I've heard so many gigs

in my mind: it's late, you look past
the whole room, your silence
inviting everyone into

your world like the talk
we never had, or those months
when performing didn't matter.

It's how I see you even now: not wanting
to play, just nudging the piano
like a rush-hour New Yorker –

hit a stray note, stare at it, wait
for the leftover sound to tell you
what tune to fall into, or who'll

survive your patience, who will leave –
wait for some polyester jacket to say,
Mr. Monk, it's really time to begin –

Those were the moods that kept us
keyed in to you more
than the elbow-dances off

the stand. Because so much
decision pressed itself into each
small move, because we wanted to say

We're listening, man, we've got the night,
and you, with your black fez & shades,
everything you didn't play.

II.

It's the silence that keeps me
awake, shaping bodies
from hanging suits,
my eyes pressed hard

to hear the crinkling night.
A Guinness, blinding
refrigerator bulb, headphones:
The London Collection

darkens my mouth to
the stout's charcoal.
Each six-note interval turns
the tune over itself like

flamed paper dancing to the chimney's
hot draw. Monk for a moment
holds on to his melody, then
breaks it: a blackened brick

cracked to its red core,
the building's plasterless skeleton
against the sky's blue sound.
What's left of the penitentiary

downtown rusts and glows
in the afternoon's warmth, iron
filings and brick paths
where men used to sing

the lives they never wanted.
Froth drips my foot
alive, eyes slowly
aware of the porch screen, the room

lit into a daguerreotype. Your silver
face, unfocused, unfolding,

white-flowered cotton
gown, hand rubbing

one eye, comes to life.
The headphones slip down as
flat-fingered chords reverberate
my neck. *Come back to bed,*

and I do, roses on the sheets
rich as Monk's rising sixths,
elevating, keeping time with the morning,
the breathing, now sunlit dust.

III.

Two sleeping pills from last night
linger this morning in my body,
everything behind the beat like
Ben Webster's wheezing tenor,
a horn with holes in it.
That's him playing, isn't it?
The piano player stealing Monk
licks. It's an old cut
and Ben's been gone for years.

Outside, these heavy boots slow
me down. Rochester February:
snow so high it covers
fire hydrants. All week
I've clipped out columns,
JAZZ GREAT IN COMA, as if
the act could keep him alive.

It's much colder than the night
I drank with a dancer from the Upper
West Side. We'd been at a party,
left early, and she pulled me into
a local bar. *Two Remy Martins* –
first hard liquor I'd ever had.
She sat real close, and cognacs later
dared me to take my shoes off,
slip the wintery sidewalk
to her apartment. We could
warm our feet with a nightcap.

Nobody noticed us and I never
felt any sting of cold.
She had a new stereo, music through
hanging beads that tinkled as she danced
from room to room to "Monk's Dream,"
until she wore nothing, took my hand
and left the record playing.

But upstate New York's no Manhattan
and these boots feel heavy enough
to drown a man in a river. Downtown,
I catch a buddy of mine, his *Times*
dappled from snow and wind.
"Hey," he says, "that jazz guy
you like to talk about died last night.
I always thought you'd have to
make up a name like that."

iv

Singapore, July 4th

Banyan roots almost reach
the river where small boats
putter to shore before dark.
The Red House,
best chili crab in town
and your friends reach for sweetness,
picking apart claws, hard shells,
sucking legs that burn the throat.
If Louis Armstrong were alive
we'd celebrate his eighty-ninth birthday,
his chili voice singing
Stars fell on Alabama.
No reason to miss the States
but I do. Tonight, back home,
when the sun begins to set on Cranes Beach,
the old mansion in the dunes
will send off Roman candles.
To Dixieland and Southern blues
floating across the seascape,
men in tuxedos will put down their Scotch,
hold their wives by the waist –
the way I'd want to be with you,
until my black suit faded into night,
your white dress only a vague glow
under chandeliers of bursting sky.

Premonitions of Sangsit

Days before we left, I thought of black
sands, turquoise shorelines,
the pink sandstone temple at Sangsit

where angular stone tigers
surround open courtyards, stonecut
sunflowers ancient as the jawless birds

lining walls and square-faced towers.
I had heard of this, but the sketch
of what I hoped to see became

the saffron dress of a young girl
who offered flowers for your hair,
took you across a trestle where

mynah birds scan the fields,
returning to rest on frangipani trees.

Except for a family by the snake-
guarded entrance of small donations,
we arrived at Sangsit alone.

No shoreline, but the sandstone
spires carved the sky while a cow
slept in the banana tree's shade.

The grass smelled too dry
and ready for rain, the way children
ask for money without asking.

One five-year-old girl followed us
through the courtyard of tigers,
tugged at our clothes, and it wasn't

until we were home I realized
she'd filled our pockets with hibiscus.

The Long Walk

Somewhere nearby, rice fields burn,
the smell of smoldering straw
blowing around a young girl
who follows the harvested perimeter.
She's balancing a round yellow basket
on her head, scarlet parasol
swinging at her side. Losing her

briefly in the trees, I reach
for the telephoto, slip it
into place and follow her sway
through thick branches. Hard
not to think a dozen years ago
she could have been a target
or a soldier's afternoon lover.

The girl steps into a circle of sun.
Framed now, in focus, panning
each step, I'm waiting for instinct
and chance as the parasol stretches open
behind her basket, the mossy wall
a soft backdrop, her shoulders
turned, a bit more, one brown eye –

I won't know for days
if I've caught her or the green path
which might take us to a marketplace
where she can sell what's in her basket:
her family's woven cloth
or fruit that ripens as she walks.

Il Cristo velato

– San Severo, Naples

Alabaster body on its back,
under a cloth thin as water
as though the artist poured
liquid stone: *The Veiled Christ.*
But I'd been told of something else,

a red arrow down the church's spiral
staircase where slaves of a Roman alchemist,
who could clot and petrify blood,
still stood – a man and a woman
who drank what he offered, and I could only hope

they died instantly. The woman
had ears, her pregnant belly bulging
outward, and, as if to prove her human,
some curator or clergyman had carved a hole
to expose her now-discolored heart.

What I asked myself then is what
I ask myself now: Did they love
each other, how much did they know,
does it matter? Perhaps,
and if they needed that moment

I want to believe they had it. So often
the mind sends internal signals
one can't explain by science,
the way some women just know
if they're carrying a boy, a girl.

Isis

– for a woman in Don Muang Airport

She began as though I knew her
or had known her long enough to care
for her lover lost in wilderness,
northern Thailand, a decade ago.
He and three others, drunk
from fermented palm sap, backpacked
into poppy fields, opium tribes.
Weeks later, only one found
in a village: crawling, mute, crazed.
Now thirty and home in Holland,
he sweats through sleep, waking
to his eyes dilated like black opals.

For the third time that year,
she will call her lover's name amid
the musty roots of banyan trees: a duffel bag
of photographs, sketches of how old
he might look, a beard, long hair.
I wanted so much to tell her,
Believe what you know is true. Instead,
I held her hands. *Good-bye.* In Amsterdam
right now, there are still four hours
before sunlight. An aging mother wipes
her son's hot face. Across the world
a younger woman rests her voice,
leans against a tree to read the leaves.

Summerhouse Piano

As though squeaks in the piano were not enough, a mouse
gave birth to her litter between the wooden center boards,

unreachable. Nothing could damage that ivory
upright, a yard-sale item dumped in my room by default,

but I had trouble sleeping with those high sounds. My step-
mother tried to drive them out with a few crippled strains

of "Maple Leaf Rag," and it left me with more admiration
for the mice: they could survive anything. That night,

the chirps more insistent, the life of their mother doubtful,
I wondered if perpetual noise would make them leave, a player

piano with an endless scroll, the ones played by four hands,
not two, though a boy can't tell by looking. It's like the story

of blind Art Tatum hearing those old scrolls before he knew
the instrument, and figuring, *That's the way it's got to sound.*

I tried humming his solo from "All God's Chillun Got Rhythm"
but it moved too fast, traveled into my head like a movie:

Art's round gut near the keys, how he'd lean back, flash
his Steinway-smile, roll through the fields, brushfire on dry

pine needles. I saw him sitting at our off-white piano, laughing
at keys that wouldn't come back up, but dealing with them:

special runs around the quirks, long lines driving the way
the force of a swollen river can push a fallen tree down-

stream, the massive trunk cascading forward in its current.

Ruby, My Dear

Swept to the bank of the Ganges,
what seemed to be charred wood
were flies clustering a child.

A sin to push it in the water?
I wasn't sure, and left the face
to its slow dissolve. It took hours

walking home, dust darkening
my feet to the sandals' leather.
Perhaps the mynah birds would tug

long enough at the tattered wrap
to thread their nests with cotton.
Ruby, what would you have said to me,

that it was the child's choice?
That sounds like you, purple shadow
under your eyes like the stretch of beach

where we'd walk, low tide reflecting
bracelets, crescent shell earrings,
necklace of lapis moons.

Didn't you once say *We choose our lives*?
If you were here in Benares you'd turn on
Thelonious with Hawkins on tenor –

This is for me, you used to say
as though Monk were your friend –
then close your eyes,

open them, look into mine:
The grief you feel is only
your own. You got away

with lines like those, sent me
on the dirt path home, crickets
making the sound of stars.

On August afternoons, you'd lay on
the horn of your red "Cropduster,"
tell me it was time to cruise

the shoreline, for cool salt air,
Monk improvising in the backseat.
I'm going to steal you from your father,

you'd tell me, *but you can call him*
from Tibet. I felt old enough to love
someone your age, though I'm grateful

you knew better, let me off easy.
And I've remembered how you wanted
to be left in the Ganges with Mingus,

but today, clouding the river
with your ashes, I felt only loss
until I smelled in this teak house

your tarot room, the Celtic cross
that brought you to the North
where the man who sells mutton

mouths your name. Perhaps you know this
and have already taken the child
to a world of sandalwood

while the earth feeds itself.
Do you remember Hawk's huge sound,
trying to guess what tree he played?

It could be any of those outside
my window – mango, coconut, Ashoka.

Blues Knowledge

Rain fizzles to electric portraits
of dazzling glitter and soot
as whorls of sparkled static shade
a flock of pigeons that circle
the cupola where stained glass
from a fire in the pews expanded
and blasted to the pavement
rosettes and shields
long since swept to the gutters
to grind in the silt of the Hudson
stirring now from a Southern hurricane's
humid tumult of newspapers and necklaces
silhouetted against cherry trees
far above this unimaginable city below
where the worn yellow lines
like unboarded bathhouses
hold no one from leaning into death
as if our eyes could summon those lights
that always turn the same bend
before machinery blossoms
and children hold their ears
and the crowd shifts awkwardly
into this time of need
so desperate in its planetary pull
no one allows himself to feel
beyond the urgent discomfort of steam
that slicks hair to the skull
until despair becomes the steel bolts
blurring perfect circles to ovals and sinking
into paint thicker than most lives
and browner than cave paintings

or dogs from Lenox Avenue
and everything tenants kill
to purify apartments or boulevards
which is why this man dragging
tin and plastic knows for sure only that
his token had a hole in its center the way I
know this train will take me
not to my wife and child
but to the blues knowledge of departure
that makes everyone stand in sweat
and turn strangely now to watch
a huge woman bespangled
in a full-length dress and cushioned beret
the color of cranberries in ginger ale
as she loops her microphone cord
and clicks the cassette into its groove
of Mississippi guitar
over the backbeat of Aretha's gospel
singing Can't find nobody like you
to another who could be her sister
but stands with tears so full and fluid
her cheeks reflect the scarlet sequins
and beside me the man's black bags
bloom into silver stamens as he raises
both palms into fingers and fists
and fingers blinking amen
and honey you've got to believe me
when I tell you on this platform
of people all living
in this city of got-to-get-there-yesterday
half of us let our trains roll on by

About the Author

Sascha Feinstein has published poems and essays in magazines and journals such as *American Poetry Review, North American Review, Crazyhorse, The Southern Review,* and *Ploughshares.* He is co-editor (with Yusef Komunyakaa) of *The Jazz Poetry Anthology* and its companion volume *The Second Set,* and the author of two critical books, including *Jazz Poetry: From the 1920s to the Present.* He is Associate Professor of English at Lycoming College in Williamsport, Pennsylvania, where he co-directs the Creative Writing Program and edits *Brilliant Corners: A Journal of Jazz & Literature.*

Copper Canyon Press wishes to acknowledge the support of Lannan Foundation in funding the publication and distribution of exceptional literary works.

LANNAN LITERARY SELECTIONS

W.S. Merwin, *The First Four Books of Poems*

Maxine Kumin, *Always Beginning: Essays*

Sascha Feinstein, *Misterioso*

John Balaban, *Spring Essence: The Poetry of Ho Xuan Huong*